NINETY-SEVEN POSTS

with the

HEADS

of

DEAD MEN

by

NANCY DEMBOWSKI

&

TORTOISESHELL · BLACK · TORONTO

© Nancy Dembowski 1998

FIRST EDITION

All rights reserved. No part of this publication may be reproduced in any manner whatsoever without written permission from the publisher, except by a reviewer who wishes to quote brief passages for inclusion in a review.

Some of these poems have been published in *Oversion, fascist panties, Torque, Queen Street Quarterly*, *Carnival: A Scream in High Park Reader* (Insomniac Press), *Understatement: An Anthology of Twelve Poets* (Seraphim Editions), and on the *Word Up* CD (Virgin Records). "74 Fears" appeared in a chapbook from n-1.

CANADIAN CATALOGUING IN PUBLICATION DATA

Dembowski, Nancy, 1956–
   Ninety-seven posts with the heads of dead men

Poems.
ISBN 1-896901-07-7

I. Title.

PS8557.E466N56 1998   C811'.54   C98-930808-1
PR9199.3.D452N56 1998

TORTOISESHELL & BLACK
22 Walmer Rd. #307
Toronto, Ontario
M5R 2W5
http://www.purefusion.com/bri/t&b.html

for

my parents

my children

bill kennedy

and

Beth Learn

Table of Contents

- 9   XXXII
- 10   The Princess and the Panopticon
- 11   The Image
- 12   I-II
- 19   III
- 20   Mirror Writing
- 21   IV
- 22   Weaving Blind
- 34   V
- 35   Borders
- 37   Fragment
- 38   The Woman Who Loved to be Tortured
- 39   VII
- 40   How to Make a Bomb
- 43   The Disembodied Poet of St. Benedict's
- 46   PlusZero
- 47   Two Forgettings
- 48   A Strange Chorus of Delicate Voices Talking Together
- 49   pome written when playing with word magnets in the basement of tower records while waiting to hear how *+0* sold
- 50   74 Fears
- 48   Sweets
- 52   LXXVI
- 54   The King's Daughter
- 55   Artificial Limbs for Sale
- 58   XIII
- 61   notes

XXXII

Dear Judge Johnson:

For civilizing the indians, the following has been successful: first, to raise cattle whereby to acquire a sense of the value of property; second, arithmetic to compute that value; thirdly writing, to keep accounts (and it is here they begin to labour: i.e., enclose farms, and the women to weave and spin); fourth, to read *Aesop's Fables*, which are their first delight along with *Robinson Crusoe*. Creeks, Cherokees, the latter now instituting a government.

It is necessary to keep them down by hard labour, poverty, ignorance, and to take from them, as from bees, so much of their earnings as that unremitting labour shall be necessary for them to obtain a sufficient surplus barely to sustain a scant life. And these earnings we apply to maintain our privileged orders in splendour and idleness and to fascinate in the eyes of the people as to an order of superior beings.

~ Thomas Jefferson
June 12, 1723

The Princess and the Panopticon

There was once upon a time a Princess
who, high under the battlements in her castle,
had an apartment with twenty-six windows,
which looked out in every possible direction.
And when she climbed up to it, and looked around her,
she could inspect her whole kingdom.
When she looked out of the first,
her sight was more keen than that of any other human being.
From the second, she could see still better.
From the third, more distinctly still.
And so it went on
until the twenty-sixth,
from which she saw everything above the earth
and under the earth
and nothing at all could be kept secret from her.
Moreover, as she was haughty and would be subject to no one
but wished to keep the dominion for herself alone,
she caused it to be proclaimed that no one should ever be her husband
who could not conceal himself from her so effectually
that it should be quite impossible for her to find him.
He who tried this, however, and was discovered by her,
was to have his head struck off and stuck on a post.
Ninety-seven posts with the heads of dead men were already standing
before the castle
and no one had come forward for a long time.
The Princess was delighted,
and thought to herself,
"Now I shall be free as long as I live."

The Image

Widows breed a web of witches.
Ghosts rise up and weave them.
The robot is outsmarted.
Crowds of people dance in zeros.
There is no faith outside of women.

I – II

gun sales lead to more gun sales
they do not clutter the market for gunnery
there is no saturation
>   ~ *Ezra Pound*

And I went down
There in the yard
Down deep
Down where they machine cotton
Right down among the seeds
Way down
So the bloodhounds would not find me.

>   And in that place
>   I lay down to sleep
>   And as I slept
>   I dreamed a dream

>   And behold . . .

I saw a man:
Clothed with rags
Standing in a certain place
With his face from his own house
A great burden on his back
And books in his hands.

>   He opened one book
>   And then another
>   And from these books came forth an image of the sea
Turned to blood like the blood from a corpse
And on this sea there sailed a ship of fools,
              A drunken boat

Laden with: gold and silver,
Jewels and pearls,
Cloths of purple and scarlet, silks, embroidered linens,
                              Designer dresses,
A lamb, with the marks of slaughter upon her,
Slaves, and the lives of men
Caught up in the body of the sea
Lost from its natural movement in the abyss of perpetual darkness.

While standing at a distance,
                    Crying out in horror

The sea-captains, voyagers, sailors, and merchant princes
Who gained their wealth
From trading on this bloody sea.

When a shadow
Came over all the ocean.

All was dark and silent.
The black shadows thrown by the moonlight
Full of a silent misery of their own
And the sea-captains, voyagers, sailors and merchant princes
Raised their arms and their voices
And sang a prayer to a name known to none but themselves
And as they sang they made a cross
And beneath the cross they affixed a shield
And above this shield they placed a wooden board
And on this board they engraved

With

                LARGE GOTHIC LETTERS

        "He was fortunate.
                        He killed a king."

        A thin mist began to creep up from the river,
It grew, and grew,
Till soon a dense fog enveloped the ship
And all those on the shore about her.
And out of the mist came the sound of hell-hounds barking,
Men stamping overhead,
The creaking of a chain,
The loud tinkle, as the check of the capstan falls into the ratchet.
And out of this misty dunghill
Gathered that sack of reptiles.

        Like night-birds of ill omen
        Crawling forth one by one
        Poisoning and to poison
        Islands, provinces undiscovered
        Yet rich in gold, silver, spices and drugs.

The very moonlight seemed alive with grisly shapes
Every speck of dust that whirls in the wind:
A devouring monster in embryo
A bloody ocean spitting out the bowels of mother earth
Bloodhounds creeping into her womb
Filthy rich with the smell of infant blood
Birthing misfits
And carrying off the souls of men.

        And are those *her* ribs through which the sun does peer?
        And is that Woman all her crew?
        Is that a Death? And are there two?
        Is Death that woman's mate?

Abandon ship
        The ship is lost
        To prayers, to prayers
                    All lost!
Yet far from the bloody ocean,
On a cold morning,
Or a damp evening,
Down a subterranean passage,
In the gloomy rooms of the old convent,
In the church of St. Nicholas,
Alone and praying at his tomb
Burning sealing wax

        And weeping at a distance

The landscape changes three times.
The sky opens twice.
And in the heart of Paris,
Loplop brings food to the street lamps,
An immaculate conception of the tenderest youth;
The great St. Nicholas
Reading fables to the children
Reading from a scroll
Embossed with human faces:
The seal, seven crowns in gold and silver
The paper, threaded thin as hair
Thin as the hair of a delicate child
Cut from Lion's teeth scissors
And the sound of wings like the noise of horses
And the ending   a rushing to battle
And every living thing in the sea
        Every living thing
        Dead.
        Dead as a doornail.

The winepress was trodden outside the city
                            And for two hundred miles around,
                  (From the press to the height of the horses' bridles)
Was the flowing of blood
The flowing of madness
And out of this red rubbish
Came crawling a vile serpent
Her tortured eyes affixed with anguish,
Writhing upon the filthy ground
Her huge knotted tail with its mortal sting
Whipping a thousand ill-formed young one's sucking at her poisoned dugs.

                      And from the mouth of this dragon,
                          The mouth of this beast,
           The mouth of this serpent prison-house:
A noisy mob of men and dogs,
Charging to either flank,
Crushing and rooting up the undergrowth around them
To the sound of M16A1 rifles, M203 grenade launchers,
M60 machine guns, M72A2 antitank weapons, M190 subcaliber devices,
M73 rockets, M18A1 claymore mines, NATO markers, Warsaw pact markers,
Vomit full of books and papers, aerial bombers dragged by the hair
                      And reaching up to the heavens
Crowding the burning temples,
Holding there, while still they could:
Their ancient images,
Their country's gods.
Till the victors grab them
A spoil that men might envy.
"Damnable, destructive, deceitful woman
  Rid yourself of all feeling of pity. We must annihilate the Jew.
  Nigger, gook, chink, faggot, bitch, slut, bum . . ."

With economics   no picture is made to endure
    But is made to sell and sell quickly
With economics   bread is ever stale
    Bread is dry as paper
With economics   the stonecutter is kept from his stone
    The weaver is keep from her loom
With economics   the child is slain in the womb

        Economics,   the false prophet,
    Impenetrable as the ignorance of old men.

    Keep awake then
        For you never know
        The day
           Or the hour.

           And it rained all night long
And in the morning, under the tent flaps, the smell of mint
And it rained, deep and heavy
And there is wind space and rain space
And flashes of lightening
An earthquake so violent the great city split in three
And all the great cities of the world fallen into endless ruin
A storm so violent

    Every island vanished
    Mountains became plains
    The earth vomited up the dead
    Bones tumbled out of tombs
    Stars fell from the sky
    The earth caught fire

And before day's end
> A whole day's wage for a quart of flour

And we went down
Into the sun burned black
To the souls of those who had been slaughtered
Into the hole
> Again.

III

There were steps before the white pigment sequestered the apple:
    murdered swimmers left over stripped presses,
        drear waste made the little gallery over the gate.

Valencia remarked before the fallen:
    "The leaves are voices."

"Help," voices whisper over the lake. "The brokers beat the seals."
    The Cedars speak:
        "There were those the year
        Raquel left the towers,
    one upturned reading breaking the seal,
        twenty peacocks shed their silvery turquoise eyes.

Get the brokers, waste the pigment, face the fallen apple, feed the nipple,
    bowe over the nipple.

The stone plaster flakes Mantegna painted are tatters."

Mirror Writing

for Aigli Papentonopolou

I have begun to live in fear of nothing,
certain my death has been revealed to me,
pouncing up, paranoid,
not of ghosts, but of the sleepless,
                the literal,
and dreams of my right breast,
you finding a lump,
       the size of a small apple
you believe me now (about the numbers being transposed
and my daughter's mirror writing)
no symbol of free-floating anxiety
having joined my brother's wife,
what is left of my sister's friend,
"but she's had seven children"
and Kelly, in her wisdom,
"we must cherish that which gives us life"
both the globe and the apple of Eden,
the sickness that feeds a whole planet,
healed with radiation,
                  a figure
    [of the end] of everything . . .

IV

for John Barlow

Palace a heap boundary ANAXIFORMINGES Aurunculeia Hear Cadmus catch and flare Dawn waking Dew-haze grass pale ankles Beat beat apple nympharum goat-foot pale alternate waters shallows A black sea-foam And carved claw-foot and head an man seated Speaking And toward and cast All swallows Cabestan's heart Cabestan's heart taste shall change And toward bar Making an arch pale a and Caught swallows Actæon and a valley valley leaves leaves a-top a fish-scale Beneath beneath a ray a a spare Flaking black water Bathing and Diana white-gathered about and air air Shaking air alight fanning hair dark and waffing Shadow'd o'ershadow'd a a shatter Actæon Vidal Vidal Vidal speaking along a patch a pale hair leap Actæon Actæon stag a sheaf hair a wheat swath Blaze blaze leap Actæon along Pergusa Gargaphia Salmacis armour shakes as rains and crystal beneath gods water bearing petals at Takasago water pale sand Visages branch-tips flaming as shallow beneath glare flame cook-stall agate casing as at that Saffron sandal petals narrow Hymenæus Hymenæe Aurunculeia scarlet cast blanch-white And saying palace Shaking imperial water-jets And Hsiange collar roars earth's bag lays water calf gauze curtains camel stairs Ecbatan Danaë Danaë What hangs stream peach-trees leaves water haze bark scrapes at rafters above black water a Gray leading Jacques speak and cedars Polhonac As Thracian platter feast Cabestan Cabestan's heart Vidal Ecbatan Ecbatan Lay lay waiting rain Garonne Saave Garonne paint sa'ave sa'ave sa'ave Regina a Adige images Across Adige Stefano Madonna As Cavalcanti had Centaur's plants earth loam And arena

Weaving Blind

Closets are a complicated fear.
One that does not translate easily into opaque notions of power,
limited versions of reality
brought about by the fundamental entanglement of slave and master.
No. Here.
Men retain their power only in closets,
where they wait and listen:
hear the sounds of curlers being warmed
rolled up
into long brown hair that needs cut,
shoes
hard and noisy
in the office on Saturday,
where they hear music only if their master wants them to
and occasionally does
and they better know their music.
Fundamental power approaching every move.
And they
don't
dare
move.

Sometimes black lipstick
or a certain something:
the dungeon at the Ivy Inn,
the pictures
in *Discipline and Punish*,
a red lace dress,
unimaginative
but strictly
of this culture.
Or even less imaginative than this,
one is likely to think:
Does a rug have dignity?
Does a peace of fluff lose its fault out of factories?
Does a piece of shit count?
Perhaps I should concern myself with dinner,
or the fact that I have two dresses to last me all summer,
or that our dialectic was always non-existent
or that most of the men I know
spend more time attacking successful women
than attempting to enact any sort of social change

                        but . . .

since each power relation is in turn a complex of power relations
since each thing is taken up in a web of forces
the distinction
may seem untenable.
Complicated it is
but not untenable.
The strands of the web can be unwound.
We can follow the trajectory of a force
across its entanglements with other forces.
We can follow the trajectory of a thing
as it passes from one knot of forces to the next.
No storm ever breaks our forces.
The tempests,
that drag the giant firs and cedars up by their roots,
who snap their branches,
and break their boles,
never break the creeping vines.
They may be torn from their strongholds,
but in the young months of the summer
the vine will climb up
and cling again.
Nothing breaks it.
So is the cobweb tie
the Men of Magic see between the Indian mother and her child.
The red telephones off at the root,
voices just worm through,
a cable of blue,

        ropes bodies

who
        will not settle for less
who
        have dreamed of this all their lives.

Before she finds the solution,
she has a vision of it
the curl of some potential,
or the slope of the tangent to the curve.
A mere drop in the cup.
A mirror makes it turn
calculates its webs
spins out spectres:
writhing, weaving,
crowds of witches
dance in zeros
in wide curves,

       before they settle,

in towns, coming in gusts, round the corners, they blew:

    here

        a hat off,

    here

          lifted a veil high above a woman's head.
            Who, with difficult steps, forced her way
              against the blowing winds,

    and was returned
        to the knotting of rope
            in place of writing.

TEXTS, BY DEFINITION,
ARE FRAGMENTS IN OPEN AND ENDLESS RELATIONS
WITH ALL OTHER TEXTS:

    THE GIFT,
    FORGIVENESS,
    AND THE TRACE:

        THAT THERE ALWAYS IS
        ALTOGETHER SOMETHING OTHER THAN
                opPOSITION
        THE THEMES OF OPPRESSION
        PASSIVELY RECEIVED
        AND PRECIPITOUSLY
        COMPULSIVELY CREDITED.

Halfway up from the little harbour of sardine boats,
halfway down from groves where the thin, bitter almond pips
fatten in green-pocked pods, the three net-menders sit out
dressed in black, everybody in mourning for
the oracular ghost who dwindles on pin-legs
to a knot of laundry, with a classic bunch of sheets:
ghost of our mother and father, ghost of us,
and ghost of our dreams' children in those sheets.
A long yellow strip of embroidery rippling down the middle.
O Sagalie Tyee, my treasure, my tears, my sobs, my happy laughter . . .
take the cobweb chains that bind – make them sing to others that they may
know the falls of Lillooett
like a million cobweb strands, dashing and gleaming down the canon,
sobbing
    laughing
weeping
    calling
singing
    as she twists
her thick hair
        rapidly into a coil
its gray strands
        a veil of mist
covering the November sky,
        a many-folded veil,
so fine meshed
        that it made one density
not transparent
        but arbitrary
and dense
whose very excesses lead to an infinite number of interpretations,
fragments
without closure or resolution.

All that can come of our wish to enter or remain
in their circles
is our death.

Woven in zeros
        used as braids
        circles, who cut,
a telescope,
an escape,
roaming press fairs
insisting . . .

a systematic and vigorous attempt

> ... reversing all the changes we had achieved.
> Women were eliminated from all decision-
> making positions within the government.
> The Family Protection law was set aside.
> Childcare centers were closed.
> Abortion became illegal.
> Women were ruled unfit to serve as judges.
> The Women's Organization was declared a den of corruption.
> University women were segregated in cafeterias and on buses.
> Women who demonstrated against these oppressive rules were slandered,
> accused of immoral behavior, attacked and imprisoned.
> Opposition grew.
> Executions became a daily occurrence.

It's funny,
> the amazing power a woman has over a man
>> merely by applying lipstick
>>> And who's in the closet?

Ah, one of those,
with a theory about everything.
Yet she had liked him,
he gave off an aroma,
a whirl,

> his flexible, supple face, worked amusingly.
> He had a round forehead, good eyes, and was bald.
> The first form of which lies in that love and desire between women
and women,
are still
without
signifiers.

It was exciting this change of proportion, hung in a fretted pattern, black lace with holes. Fragments of other people's talk reached us in broken sentences.

Black and white slabs on the hall beneath,
> AHH
>> but they were useful.

>> The train rushed with a roar through the tunnel.
>> It seemed to perform and act of amputation.

>>> Cut off from that circle of light.

we spend years discussing problems of aesthetics,
debating designs and patterns,
the weight of wool
the colours of threads and yarns
the spools of mangled tears
the braids of spinning skin
the double helix
the ladder always there
the space both down and in.
                        For when we begin to give up
our fingers,
as if,
of their own accord,
begin to weave,
and as we weave
we talk and laugh and sing and curse and swear all to ourselves
and then we weave some more.
Until we begin to lace together,
one long footnote,
threading its way though the impossibility of boundaries or borderlines,
until we begin to replace a privileged origin,
with the trace of something prior:

a +0
a secret
a silence
an orphan text
an indecipherable alphabet
a ghostly language of the ancient earth
and all the long etceteras of such thought.
Fashioned on our own.
    Born from the nothingness of non-presence,

        a Frankenstein of hope.

V

smothered beneath a mule, a poet's ending
                    ~ *Ezra Pound*

Her fresh earned approaching steps.
Her streets measureless.
Her dark unguarded fire.
Her grey Pieire Thesaurus.
Her roadway for approaching rain.
Her smothered horse.
Her dreamed star-maze sea-crest.
Her girl cries.
Her uncertain friend (Brutus smothered praise beforehand).
Her feared friend, from abroad: uncertain, unguarded.
Her four men mourned before wood-barge burned yearly.
Her Barabello.
Her different run Tiber.
Her greasy afterbirth garbage.

Borders

for bill kennedy

The walls are nearly naked;
        just the edges of clean paint,
where absent pictures
frame my children
and half a dozen out-grown playthings.

We pretend to watch his composition of magnetic letters;

The B means nothing

        without the E.

Even now, we barely contain ourselves;
pushed to the corners,
you slide your hand beneath my blouse.
My breasts will miss you.
My fingers, caught between the glue and paper,
extract the letter:
        month-old mail;
in black, as though in mourning,
(I forget what shoes or dress it was exactly).
Out of shock, or habit, I entered it on disk;
as though inscribing, in memory, would erase, somehow, its meaning.
I cut out words, bits of syntax;
effaced the fable of the princess
who gained microscopic vision from
a tower with twenty-six windows.
What she wanted most was freedom.
And thus, decreed that any suitor
who could not escape her vision,
would lose his head in trying.

  97 heads stood in rows before her castle

— the border of her freedom —

And who will you construct of me from memory?
In whose imagination will you bury our existence
in patterns of your language?
Letters repelling and attracting;
little fingers move the o beneath the r and form a gibbet.
Should I say my country needs me?
They are starving out the children,
as I wait halfway the distance of indignance,
and the horror, of the bones beneath my babies.

Should I write that I am screaming?
Or absent myself from presence?
The children won't recall that we once lived here;
so I must paint for them your vision,
from the road maps of our teardrops,
in the absence of your letters,
I was always good at acting.

Fragment

Between the Peacock and the Shoe Museum
you interpret Derrida's theory as +0.
Madame de Maintenon reads the future
with a wicked pack of stalks:
"Here," she said, "the yin line of the I Ching is broken
and all these years you never noticed."
The girlfriend of situations,
in her fishnets and feathers,
frames the spaces of her bruises
etched in cybernated windows.
She looks in vain.
The receptive brings no shelter.
The creative are no rulers.

The Woman Who Loved to be Tortured

for Mary Shelley

A being, whom I myself had formed and imbued with life,
had me,
at midnight,
along the precipice of an inaccessible mountain,
and there, a multitude of filthy animals inflicted incessant torture,
extorted screams and bitter groans,
as a public indignation turned with renewed violence
toward the tortures of the accused.
Remorse tore my bosom.
A kind of insanity possessed me.
The ballots had been thrown,
the vote, little but a heap of broken images.
And it snows,
although it is the end of April.

VII

Death phantom, beneath the house, throws lamplight shadow. Shadow heavy with speech. Speech choked with ghostly things. Things weighted with British echo. Echo that mouths chronicles. Chronicles heavy with Homer. Homer then shoulders the speech that shells the house. House, thick with shells, then throws shade behind another phantom: hair, hand, cheeks, shoulders . . . death.

How to Make a Bomb

for Maurice Guilbert

Tell me, my dear Maria,
do you never retrace, in your memory, the time we passed here together?
To me it recurs forever, and yet I think I recollect a dream,
or some visionary fancy where most poets assume mercenaries
are merely bodyguards
in charge of the last eyewitness to the murder of her roommates.
She was continually repeating:

      "Please don't kill me . . .

                      please don't kill me

        too."

                      and

      "After the first one, chick,

                      the rest comes easy

                            after that."

      GOVERNMENT ASSISTANCE
            REALLY MEANS
                  GOVERNMENT CONTROL

Men,
hired en masse,
not just by governments and royalty,
but by individuals
        for defense
            and conquests.
            The original techniques
            having been found,
                in many cases,
                    too slow,
                    involved,
                    complex.

Many have racial or political aspects
explaining some of the controversy surrounding the
two oblong blocks of moulded explosive
joined together with brass bolts and recessed to contain
the metal striker assembly.

A grocer is stabbed in the second of a series of bad scenes:
a study of maps, history, statistics, photos,
how not to wind up broke, lost, or worse.
It is a simple form,
requiring only proof of your birth, current address,
a fee, a full-face photograph.
A rubber stamp, whacked, without question,
directly into your passport at the airport or border station,
       and, as affairs become strained,
            embassies are sometimes closed
                  consulates left, as the last line of communication.

All countries require permission to get in
but because she was still unable to find the runaway girl
by the end of her day's tour
she was too busy wondering if she: "shoulda stayed home washin' dishes
       or sewin' a man's socks."
A poor terrified thing in a concrete jungle,
not an animal to be whipped,
but the flesh and blood of his wife,
who advanced towards us,
with an air of assumed importance,
demanding to know
what she should explain first
and then,
only to discover,
hundreds of miles too late,
the really entertaining ones require permission to get out.

"I'll skin you alive, chick, an' use you to wipe my shoes,"
 screeches out across the dumpy downtown rooftops.
 And last night was the beginning of something,
 heading to some exotic spot not listed in the tour guide,
 canceled flights, coups, weather problems as sure as bad apples.
 And the little things that could go wrong.
 Fine print in the forged passport.
 hints at the revocation of citizenship,
 didn't even bother to ask for specifics
 question the little details
 and just now realizes part of her job is saluting another flag.
"Please don't hurt me like Loretta" plays on the jukebox.
 Only the drive home
 and she can get out of that uniform
 and go to the beach,
 where her best chances,
 in this incredibly screwed-up operation,
 consist of getting killed or captured
 before she gets so far along as to discover
 she was never likely to have been paid.

The Disembodied Poet of St. Benedict's

for Natalee Caple

The dead forty-nine year old Henry James typed mechanically. A man of great cultivation and charm, within a minute his intellectual and perceptual powers were effaced by toxic attachments. For, as he entered into relation with this machine, he functioned precisely as a machine functions. The tremendous movement of his fingers did not convey studies of life struggling against incredible adversity, but amiably carved abstract and categorical images in a nonexistent chronological order. Restless with this sublime linguistic hunger, he wandered the corridors of his right hemisphere. It was in this labyrinth of computer portals that he found himself at the mercy of absurd little professors peering and pointing with obsessed concentration.

His first perception of these grotesquely distorted phantoms lead to a bizarre state of desperate frenzy where he would spend hours jamming his deformed hand into an ill-knit glove. Completely lost to ontological fatigue, it was without the basic powers of perception that he entered into relation with the picture as a whole. He understood then that the world aesthetic was condemned to a sort of "Humean" froth, a meaningless fluttering on the surface of life, empiricism not taking account of the soul. He found this world of isolated impressions heartbreaking and was drawn to transcend the incoherence.

A broken creature, his childhood stories were to become the origin of his healing. Although he was raised by musical retardates in a variety of crowded circus wagons, scenes of joy and happiness had unconsciously emerged during Freudian analysis. Still, isolated memories of when his mother and father were running a colour-blind traffic in slavery, evoked a pathos of radical lostness. By prescribing a collusion between the powers of pathology and creation, the absurd little professors hoped to reorganize Henry. To paraphrase, they wished him to delete the details of a poignant narrative beauty and brave an inversion of the usual linguistic order of things. A trivial but rigid formalism, *in toto* with an ever-changing cultivation of details, was designed to unravel his hopelessness.

This rehabilitative instruction provided Henry with a strange and meditative calm of almost holy intensity. Out of the blue, short sentences following one another in meaningless order were no longer faulty meaningless sequences. Something closeted dared move, and, with its reckoning, he found new and fascinating qualities hidden in babble. With this exceptional feeling for language, Henry was going home. He was going back to where he came from, a place where a nonrepresentational robin redbreast lustily gave birth on a carpet of mauve clover and April foliage. In this living interplay of botanical works and bizarre species of animals, his dead brother, William, and his sister, Alice, were hand-printing exquisite Japanese lettering onto books of concrete poetry. Music stands of leatherbound manuscript codices containing records of conversations, biographical novels, and a brilliant essay on the world as forms, were organised algebraically. Scattered among this mosaic of rare texts were crumpled leaves and offprints revealing gorgeous capitals, beautiful numbers, and a fragile looking A hand-etched with minute accuracy. Henry looked for a colour Xerox.

Finding the use of a facsimile an ungrounded focus, he turned aside this nuisance and fixed his concern on an evocative gothic novel. Upon touching the manuscript, something very disquieting happened to him. His immortal soul went on a return journey to the closing years of the last century. There he typed among smutty comics and kitchen flower gardens in a hospital for the criminally insane. It was here the nightmares began.

Henry was receiving clinical reintegration at St. Benedict's asylum. At first he was intrigued, but as he came to re-experience memories of the past, a hallucinatory delirium brought him visitations from apparitions with gross amputations and lobotomies. Like a godforsaken carnival scene, the apparitions tried to tear off his face, and, failing this, had stolen into the Dissecting Room, nabbed a leg, and then slipped it under his bedclothes. He seized the creepy horrible thing with both hands, and with an extraordinary violence, tried to throw the macabre limb out of his bed. The featureless cylinder turned to chalk in his hands. Henry was covered in tissue. Tormented to the point of madness, he began screaming with terror and confusion. Suddenly the floor seemed further, then suddenly nearer, it pitched, it jerked, it tilted like a ship in heavy seas. He could hardly feel the ground beneath him and flailing to and fro he dropped into a bottomless abyss where he heard an ocean of voices, several at once and far away, rapidly singing their cruel theme: "war, violence, murder."

Whenever Henry moved, a kaleidoscopic nightmare of ever-changing ghostly figures, mutations from a world half-forgotten half-recalled, came at him from a ghastly universal darkness. He did not know what he had just done or from where he had just come. Lost in this existential labyrinth of transformations, the possibility of a grotesquely deformed species condemned to a nothing but product blindness preoccupied his thoughts. A graveyard vision of flaming falling stars told him something awful was fermenting. But then . . . with all the appearance of a man violently ill, he expelled all the gestures, the postures, the expressions, the demeanours, the entire behavioral repertoires of the seductive phantoms. Mercifully, he dreamt of a trembling poetess whose evocations enveloped him in phantasies of peaceful possibility. Thousands of cherished memories crowded suddenly into his mind, his imagination an enchanted loom weaving ever-dissolving patterns of meaning. For with this hypnotic déjà vu came the release of narrative form. Fragmentary signifiers mourning the waterhood of lyrical antiquity. A sea of symbolist allusion fossilised in Blakean tone poems dancing with the feverish topography of wished mathematics. A magical scene of loving paper, storm-tossed and mysteriously fluid.

PlusZero

And at once
Derrida's cloudburst rained vitamins
and no one took them.
Outside of this prison she has sex in a television set
and PlusZero is infantilized correctly.
But in the newspaper, deceased Madame de Maintenon
bites her nails,
for the yin line of the I Ching is broken and all these years she never noticed.

Girlfriend of situations frames the spaces of her bruises
[knitted holes of fishnet fracted onto cybernated windows]
as ghosts etch webs of witches sweeping arbitrary zeros.

Freud laughed and cast a backward glance.

Two Forgettings

I

She had had the forest cut down for him,
she had had the fish-pond cleaned out for him,
she had had the castle built for him,
she had changed him into a briar,
and then into a church,
and at last into a fish-pond,
and yet he had forgotten her so quickly.

II

I set thee free when thou wert in an iron stove in the wild forest.
I sought thee, and walked over a glass-mountain
and over three sharp swords and a great lake before I found thee,
and yet thou wilt not hear me!

III

I have followed after thee for seven years.
I have been to the sun and the moon,
and the four winds,
and have inquired for thee,
and have helped thee against the dragon;
wilt thou, then, quite forget me?
But the Prince slept so soundly that it only seemed to him
as if the wind were whistling outside in the fir trees.

A Strange Chorus of Delicate Voices Talking Together

Although she pretended to be very fond of him,
he did not dare to venture over the white circle.
She tied up her maimed arms
and went forth on her way at sunrise
where a guardian fairy appeared
as no doctor had been able to cure her of that large city watchman
and his story of a ghost in the garden.
Yesterday evening, while she was asleep,
I cut off her head, as she has only two eyes
like any common person.
Under the cellar steps a toad made a nest of her hair.
In snow-white robes from heaven came a wicked wizard
always interrupting the messengers and sending false letters
from green parrots in gilt cages gradually pining away.
He did not spoil his pleasure court
and was turned into a black poodle made to eat live coals.
And the old king
caused the wicked cook to be torn into four quarters
when apples fell like rain
and a handful of jewels grew white with anger in her handkerchief.
The fame and beauty and riches of the maiden
went all over the world
while countless glow-worms swarming fragrance echoed
just as if a sharp knife had pierced her heart.
A basket and a rope.
Lonely as any spirits of the air pictured hovering about
without stopping the shameless greedy malicious dwarf
repeatedly hammering vermin
while continuously whispering backwards and forwards,
"What will you give me if I spin all this straw into gold?"

POME WRITTEN WHEN PLAYING WITH WORD MAGNETS IN THE BASEMENT OF TOWER RECORDS WHILE WAITING TO HEAR HOW +0 SOLD

sweet scream sprayed out of her frantic moment
drunk in her language
a worshiping of wind and meat
a mad moan springing languid
she fiddles not to pedal a thousand enormous moments
for a sad apparatus about
when over why he will paint pink milk or sausage
one lazy water after sky

74 Fears

Fear God and the stupidity of the populace.
Fear the local loan lice.
Fear Barabbas minus Hemingway.
Fear that birds would not eat the white bread.
Fear the standard of living.
Fear Till, hung yesterday.
Fear the slaves learning slavery.
Fear the souls of the children.
Fear this from the monument.
Fear larceny in a regime based on [   ] larceny.
Fear more than at present.
Fear paradise at the end of it.
Fear robbing the public.
Fear the grey walls of an era.
Fear that criminals have no intellectual interests.
Fear the two largest rackets.
Fear each in the name of his God.
Fear the government which lasted.
Fear the a.h. of the army.
Fear the greek classics.
Fear (those) amused by the British.
Fear Madame Lucrezia.
Fear playing checkers with black Jim.
Fear the coffee house facts of Vienna.
Fear we who have passed over Lethe.

Sweets

for Paul Dembowski

The waiter cracks an egg:
Our salads sit.
We take the stairs.
Our room is a museum.
He's dressed his gift of chocolates in his Sunday shirt,
I wear it open and alone,
the skin of his eyes, his cheeks, sweet with aperitif
I drink quickly and think,
he is the lover of my life
        this is the most elegant room I have ever been in
                in my life.

My mother's house was simple:
butterscotch in coloured glass
no chandeliers to dress me in rainbows
only brother's prisms on the window sills
in some way equated with his love of symbols.

My husband calculates our travels:
I wait outside the door
I am mad for Japanese lanterns and American flags,
summers, thieving ice creams and pencils,
minus brother's brilliance in my hands.
Words were nothing next to numbers.

I keep my lover's chocolates in my bag
and find a place where I am close enough to watch
like a movie:
there is blood on the sidewalk
and bars on the window.
I count, to the flicker of cars,
        while his hands undress my chocolates
                and the money tumbles out.

LXXVI

I am in the kitchen, playing scrabble with Mitchell,
when I hear John, over the radio, asking me to write a poem about Jefferson
and I answer,
        that the sun,
                in her great periplum,
                      leads in her influence

and that the I Ching and the Tao Te Ching are never wrong.
        We meet at the corner,
           -   where an old woman holds a magazine
                  featuring a barefoot girl who murdered her child.

In a cage now,
        reading prejudice
                and praying for sincerity:
anything opposed to the values of bricabrac and seadrift

anything opposed to going to the cake shop
and buying some bubble gum, some stickers for his notebook.
And it was Pound who wrote so well about Jefferson:

    "in civilizing the indians the following has been successful:
      first, to raise cattle whereby to acquire a sense of the value of property,
      second, arithmetic to compute that value . . .

and here they begin to labour,"
as the rain fell all night long
and the wind blew over the place
where the three roads cross.

And in sight of the castle,
            there is wind space,
                        there is rain space,
and no more an altar to Mithras.
A sense of humour seems to prevail now
in the buying of fields in meter, yard, or measure
as there is no labouring before arithmetic.

The King's Daughter

Three brothers appeared in the palace before her sorrow:
one of them hurried to the sun,
and the last was to hide himself in two parts,
and came to a lake.
But be sure that she was alarmed, and suffered it to be proclaimed,
that one night the raven,
ordered outside to the person who could not discover her,
fetched to the surface of the heads of the water with such violence
that the bird cried in every possible direction.
One long time she would look on her blood-stained hands,
which dared not conceal from herself the days,
which had been three years, every evening, until six in the water.
Next day, she often saw everything above the earth and blood
and every window shivered, a wave rose out of her foot
and then into a thousand pieces flew all in vain.
The winds were whistling outside in the water
and as she cut the eleventh air on the ninetieth and ninety-seventh post
she meditated, at length, from the first window of the palace,
but she longer knew her light was about to break.
This consoled her, when she was haughty, and did not know where.
She looked out in flames placed on the glass-mountain.
The next day she went back
and felt the sea-hare
fighting beneath the braids of the water.

Artificial Limbs for Sale

for Beth Learn

Monsters are not sent. Once made available to the public the right of interpretation is the reader's.

Intensely preoccupied with the value of all sorts of little objects, he is going to turn the attic of his parents' house into a private apartment with bourgeois fixings. His girlfriend, a twenty-six-year-old woman who has been addicted to heroin since age sixteen, is led by the hand through pitch-dark rooms and given something he is fond of playing with. He spoke of: women's work, meticulous daily observance of God's word, physical differences between the sexes, and other wonders of nature.

Her heavy heart prevented her from answering and receiving messages from a world she once knew deeply, long since forgotten. She flung it aside (doing harm to the most delicate nerves of his body), and, at the same time, making strange motions spewing: acerbic satire, long homilies, biting mockery. That night she wrote her first poem: *Artificial limbs for sale.*

He makes note. A blessed union has taken place between the profound philosopher and the iron man of action. An ear for sophisticated and minute nuances, he never saw fit to do violence to her text. The words *cool* and *teeny-bopper* appeared on nearly every page. After a lengthy and laborious process of reconstruction, this gave him the idea of juxtaposing certain passages, attaining something with the text that either was not possible or completely superfluous. Staring with an empty gaze, demonized, sliding under the length of several beds, there was a voice within him, not based on verifiable scientific evidence but on subjective association, that would not be still. The absurdities of the graveyard of his childhood came together at once: isolation, callous indifference, houses in his arithmetic book six squares wide and four squares high.

INITIAL SYMBIOTIC RELATIONSHIP: An unmarried servant girl who slept in a cattle trough: drinker, borrower, card player, and prostitute, who always had peach juice for him, never learned to talk right, and has to be beaten even now to get off sexually.

LACK OF A SATISFYING SYMBIOSIS GUARANTEES IDEALIZATION OF A NARCISSISTICALLY CATHECTED COLLECTIVE GRANDIOSITY: Cutting into little pieces, cutting off of limbs, decapitation, castration, putting out the eyes, slicing section of flesh from buttocks and thighs (which he then smelled) and unsuccessful attempts at anal intercourse with his stuffed animals.

THEATRICAL GESTURES: He sometimes put on a performance for the cat.

LACK OF OBJECT CONSTANCY: A series of maids die alone in a stinking john.

Found sitting among the ruins, mother tried to put a stop to her son's games. Ever since she discovered sister doing it, she was leaving no stone unturned. Dolls constantly being beaten. Little girls choked on the playground. (It was obvious she would have trouble in her relationships with men.) He suddenly reappears on the lovely parquet floor.

REASON CONSTITUTES ONLY A SMALL PART OF BEING: Our capacity to resist has nothing to with our intelligence but with the degree of access to our true self. She took off her T-shirt. He pushed his hand down inside the back of her pajamas.

IRRATIONAL WISHFUL THINKING: A real friend would be sure to reach inside his pants.

RULES OF THE GAME: Humiliation can be of help here. Feigning friendliness helps even more. She doesn't have to call him Uncle Richard anymore.

The sun does not need to be told to shine (careless hands remember similar scenes with men more closely related). She reached inside his pants.
Ajax, the dog, intervened.

THE IMPORTANCE OF LOSS OF OBJECT: Use of a lifeless human body: docile, malleable, obedient, Paul Klee made wonderful puppets.

She tried to escape. Groping in the dark labyrinth, alone with her suffering and far more dependent than her pride would like to admit, she can't ever remember being affectionate... nothing more, nothing more... she doesn't want, she can't, she couldn't... an antiseptic impression unreal somehow... wants something from her ... far off in another room ... and wants something from her. That is why she exists. No need to have dreams. The black wall will rage over and burn, burn, burn ....

Ajax got terribly nervous.

In order to calm down he killed her hamster before her eyes and cut it into selected and juxtaposed pieces. The despised food attempts to coerce orgies of gluttony followed by vomiting. Fingers are thicker and fleshier.

Anchored in uncritical loyalty, she endures extreme torment mortally afraid at the thought of him leaving her. Her compartment on the train waited at the train station.

CRITICAL PREREQUISITE OF SYMPATHY IS MISSING: Seriously deranged, such a person can be used for practically any purpose: psychoses, drug addiction, criminality.

THE NEED TO FIND AN OUTLET FOR REPRESSED AFFECT: *Long as you're here you might as well get into bed with me.*

REPETITION COMPULSION: He expressed the wish to live near his mother. Manipulated by various forms of propaganda, he was led astray by the intensity of his true feelings and finally overcome with such hearty, violent and uncontrollable laughter that he smothered and died.

Overnight she advocates views totally different from those held the day before. She got out his doll carriage, locked the apartment door behind her and went for a walk collecting cigarette butts from trash cans (a container into which we can safely throw all our emotional garbage) and turned somersaults until she collapsed on the playground.

XIII

Confucius departs
> from the second gate
> and goes in the direction,
> of the path of many windings,

And with this enlightened leader is T'ung, Jàn
> and the one strong man among many

And "we stand confronting one another," says Confucius,
"Warm attachment that springs from the heart is lacking?
> Is there is but one persevering nature in this society,
"Or are all equally close to one another?
"No divergent aims have yet arisen?"
And Ch'ien says, "Secret agreements bring humiliation,"
And T'ung says, "Fellowship should not be mere mingling - this would be chaos."
And Jàn says, "It is not the private interests of the individual,
"that create lasting fellowship among persons,
> "but rather the goals of humanity,"

And the strong man among many arranged words freely
Mingling forms that pour forth
> like the fragrance of orchids,

And flame up to heaven,
And that is why it is said:
> "Low motives lead,

"In the course of time to misfortune,
"the meadow is the pasture at the entrance to the town."
> And Confucius is welcoming to all.

And Li says with concern:
> "Is a heavy burden shut away in silence?"

And Confucius says, "Two people are outwardly separated,
"But in their hearts they are united."
And Confucius distrusts Shih,
> Shih is of low character,

For Shih gives the idea of fellowship
> but plans a secret ambush.
And Confucius says
> "For three years he does not rise up,
But hides weapons in the thicket."
> And Confucius says
"In order to hold together a peaceful union of men
"A persevering leader is needed,
"A man with clear and convincing aims
> And the strength to carry them out."
And "When the superior man has arranged a formation
The strength of creative words will succeed at this time."
And Confucius said, and bound the words:
> If a man has no order within
He cannot originate order without;
And if a man is without inner order
His fellowship with men will not be in order;
> And if the superior man has no order within
He cannot bring order to mankind.
And Confucius gives the words "order"
and "fellowship with men"
And has reservations with "the nature of heaven."
And he said
> "True fellowship among persons are not exclusive,
The basic principals of any kind of union,
Must be accessible to all concerned."

And they said: If a thoughtful man leads a warlike army yet cannot surprise his opponent
> Must we shut away the danger and ally ourselves with him?
And Confucius said:
> We must ally ourselves with him.

And Confucius is true to Jàn-Li
> When Jàn-Li has mental difficulties.
And he gives sweet words to Ch'ien T'ung
> when Ch'ien T'ung is outwardly mistrustful.

And Confucius said "Li T'ung seeks the image of the heart,
        A community of people,
With the strength of bronze
And the sweet fragrance of warm attachment,
Remaining true to each other,
When obstacles arise between them."
And Confucius said, "When cross words pour freely forth
        even people who dwell near one another
Are kept apart by this diversity.
The fragrance of orchids
        runs in the direction of the meadow
arranged organically with the luminaries in the sky."

Notes

Ninety-Seven Posts with the Heads of Dead Men is, in part, an exploration of the relationship between the literal and the allusory. Readers interested in investigating this aspect of these poems may want to examine them in relation to the following texts:

XXXII
Pound, Ezra. *The Cantos.* Canto XXXII.

The Princess and the Panopticon
Grimm, Jakob and Wilhelm. "The Sea-Hare." *The Complete Household Tales of Jakob and Wilhelm Grimm.*

I-II
Bunyan, John. *The Pilgrim's Progress: In The Similitude of a Dream.*
Coleridge, Samuel Taylor. "The Rime of the Ancient Mariner."
Dickason, Olive P., and L.C. Green. *The Law of Nations and the New World.*
Drew, Benjamin. *The Refugee: or the Narratives of Fugitive Slaves in Canada.*
Ernst, Max. *The Hundred Headless Woman (La femme 100 têtes).*
Foucault, Michel. *Madness and Civilization: A History of Insanity in the Age of Reason.*
Homer. *The Iliad.* Book XII.
Keats, John. "Lamia."
Milton, John. *Paradise Lost.* Books I, II.
The New English Bible. Matthew; Revelation.
Ovid. *Metamorphoses.* Book XIII.
Otway, Thomas. [Excerpted in Bartlett's *Familiar Quotations.*]
Pound, Ezra. *The Cantos.* Cantos I, XLV, LXXIV, XCIX.
Shakespeare, William. *The Tempest.*
Shirer, William L. *The Rise and Fall of the Third Reich: A History of Nazi Germany.*
Spenser, Edmund. *The Faerie Queen.*
Stoker, Bram. *Dracula.*
Terrell, Carroll F. *A Companion to the Cantos of Ezra Pound.*
U.S. Military. *Soldier's Manual of Common Tasks.*

Walpole, Horace. *The Castle of Otranto.*
Ward, Chas. A. "Epistle to Henry II"; "Historical Fragments." *Oracles of Nostradamus.*

III
Pound, Ezra. *The Cantos.* Canto III.

IV
Pound, Ezra. *The Cantos.* Canto IV.

Weaving Blind
Afkhami, Mahnaz, qtd. in Marilyn Waring, *If Women Counted: A New Feminist Economics.* Chapter 8.
Brogan, T. F., and Alex Preminger, eds. "Intertextuality." *The New Princeton Encyclopedia of Poetry and Poetics.*
Derrida, Jacques. *Given Time: I. Counterfeit Money.* Chapter 2.
Hejinian, Lyn. *My Life.*
Irigaray, Luce. *The Irigaray Reader.* Chapters 4, 5.
Johnson, E. Pauline. "The Legend of Lillooet Falls." *The Moccasin Maker.*
Learn, Beth. *In the Laboratory of the Psychologist.*
Massumi, Brian. *A User's Guide to Capitalism and Schizophrenia: Deviations from Deleuze and Guattari.*
Philip, Marlene Nourbese. *Looking for Livingstone: An Odyssey of Silence.*
Plath, Sylvia. "Daddy"; "The Ghost's Leavetaking"; "The Net-Menders."
Rich, Adrienne. "Diving into the Wreck"; "Phantasia for Elvira Shatayev." *Fact of a Doorframe.*
Tsu, Lao. *Tao te Ching.* Eighty.
Woolf, Virginia. *The Years.* 1911, 1914, 1918.
Wordsworth, William. *The Prelude.* Books 2, 8, 11.

V
Pound, Ezra. *The Cantos.* Canto V.

The Woman Who Love to be Tortured
Eliot, T. S. *The Waste Land.*
Shelley, Mary. *Frankenstein.*

VII
Pound, Ezra. *The Cantos.* Canto VII.

How to Make a Bomb
Buckley, S. *The Mercenary's Survival Manual.*
Burney, Fanny. *Evelina.* Vol. II, Letter x.
DC Comics. *Lady Cop* (1st Issue Special).
US Military. *Booby-Traps.*

The Disembodied Poet of St. Benedict's
Sacks, Oliver. *The Man Who Mistook His Wife for a Hat and other Clinical Tales.*

Two Forgettings
Grimm, Jakob and Wilhelm. "The Iron Stove"; "The Singing, Soaring Lark"; "The Two Kings' Children." *The Complete Household Tales of Jakob and Wilhelm Grimm.*

A Strange Chorus of Delicate Voices Talking Together
Grimm, Jakob and Wilhelm. *The Complete Household Tales of Jakob and Wilhelm Grimm.* Volume 1.

74 Fears
Pound, Ezra. *The Cantos.* Canto LXXIV.

LXXVI
Pound, Ezra. *The Cantos.* Cantos XXXII, LXXVI.

The King's Daughter
Grimm, Jakob and Wilhelm. "The Sea-Hare." *The Complete Household Tales of Jakob and Wilhelm Grimm.*

Artifical Limbs for Sale
Miller, Alice. *For Your Own Good: Hidden Cruelty in Child-Rearing and the Roots of Violence.*

XIII
Wilhelm, Richard and Cary S. Baynes, trans. *The I Ching or Book of Changes.* Hexagram 13.

Acknowledgments

COVER ART:	Tara Azzopardi
AUTHOR PHOTO:	Steve Venright
COVER DESIGN:	Natalee Caple and Brian Panhuyzen
EDITING:	Natalee Caple
COPYEDITING:	Darren Wershler-Henry
DESIGN AND TYPOGRAPHY:	Brian Panhuyzen
PRINTING:	Coach House Printing, Toronto
DISTRIBUTION:	Marginal Distribution, Peterborough

The author wishes to thank the following for inspiration and support:

Mahnaz Afkhami Wendy Agnew Gordon Michael Allen Tara Azzopardi Louise Bak Nikki Barbier John Barlow Jill Battson Christian Bök daniel f. bradley Allen Breismaster T.V.F. Brogan Shirley Buckley Nancy Bullis John Bunyan Arthur Burgess Barbara Burgess John Burgess Violet Burgess Monika Burkehardt Fanny Burney Stephen Cain Natalee Caple Victor Coleman Samuel Taylor Coleridge Mark Connery Kelly Dembowski Mitchell Dembowski Paul Dembowski Jacques Derrida Olive P. Dickason David Donnell Benjamin Drew Nicky Drumbolis Paul Dutton T.S. Eliot Max Ernst Tamara Fairchild Laura Fine Michel Foucault Denise George Kelly Lynn Grace L.C. Green Josephine Grey Jakob and Wilhelm Grimm Maurice Guilbert Lyn Hejinian all the hippies michael holmes Homer Rachele Hosten Stephen Humphrey Frederick Innis Luce Irigaray Gayle Irwin Alice Miller Pauline Johnson Clifton Joseph Adeena Karasick John Keats bill kennedy Pierre L'Abbé Beth Learn Joy Learn Peggy Leffler Alexandra Leggat Jill Lowery Luba Brian Massumi Diane Mason Steve McCabe Peter McPhee John Milton Candy Minx Onuphrio Muralto Tanya Nanavanti Nedra Jim Nightshade Mike O'Conner Thomas Otway Ovid David Owen Brian Panhuyzen Steven Pender Kathy Pereira Marlene Nourbese Philip Sylvia Plath Coman Poon Ezra Pound Alex Preminger Richard Preston Adrienne Rich Stan Rogal Kelly Ryan Lisa Ryder Oliver Sacks William Shakespeare Mary Shelley William L. Shirer Edmund Spenser Bram Stoker Carroll F. Terrell Helen Tsiriotakis Lao Tsu Steve Venright Chas. A. Ward Marilyn Waring Darren Wershler-Henry Maureen White Ivan Brian Wilson Virginia Woolf William Wordsworth Sue Young Jeremy Zeitlin Suzanne Zelazo

7880021